Prayers for the Heart of the
SINGLE GODLY WOMAN

FOOD FOR THE SOUL OF THE SINGLE GODLY WOMAN

Single Ladies in Christ

NANCY ALLENDER

authorHOUSE®

AuthorHouse™
1663 Liberty Drive
Bloomington, IN 47403
www.authorhouse.com
Phone: 1 (800) 839-8640

Published by AuthorHouse   01/08/2019

ISBN: 978-1-5462-7281-6 (sc)
ISBN: 978-1-5462-7280-9 (e)

Library of Congress Control Number: 2018914832

Print information available on the last page.

Introduction

I Thessalonians 5:17 (KJV)

Pray without ceasing.

Prayers give us a direct connection to our Father. It is a way of personally communicating our thoughts, needs and desires to Him; talking to our Creator. Also an opportunity to offer praise and thanksgiving unto Him.

Being single and Godly, we have special needs that can only be fulfilled by God. Single Godly women have heartfelt desires that because of our singleness, can only be met by Him and I know, because I am one. God also has a special calling on single Godly women...assignments that can only be filled more easily because of our singleness. Remember Jesus was single when He walked this earth and I truly believe that was just so he could more easily fulfill the purpose God had on his life. He had His hands full dealing with the disciples, let alone a wife!

During this single season in our lives, it gives us an opportunity to lean in and push into the Father for a closer one on one relationship with Him. Being single, we also learn strength and courage which often comes out of necessity, but we must still be humbled and learn to be still and listen to the Father's voice of direction. This type of "Godly flexibility" can only come from being single in Him. We talk to Him in prayer, but also must learn to listen to Him and obey His wisdom for our life. Then we move forward in what He would have for our single lives in Him.

Allow these prayers to be a blessing to your single Godly soul! Embrace them and cherish them with the thought that they were written specifically for you with your Godly single heart in mind.

You are your Father's daughters and He loves you and wants nothing for you but what is true, righteous and virtuous. Allow this book to bring you closer to Him by making time to talk to Him and use it in your everyday single life to experience him often. May God bless you and strengthen you in doing so.

You will notice some scriptures are repeated, however they were given to me to insert in certain sections as a reminder; the repetition in the scriptures are deliberate as to keep you mindful of God's promise to you. Be Blessed!

Philippians 4:6, 7 (KJV)

Be careful for nothing; but in every thing by prayer and supplication with thanksgiving let your requests be made known unto God. And the peace of God, which passeth all understanding, shall keep your hearts and minds through Christ Jesus.

About The Book

Use this book as "Spiritual Recharging" for your single soul; let the prayers wash over your spirit when you're needing to be recharged as all us ladies need from time to time. Keep it handy; keep it close!

These prayers were given to me by the Holy Spirit to share with you to offer your single heart, comfort, peace, contentment and to dispel your feelings of loneliness with all scriptures being taken from the King James Version of the Bible.

These writing will help you in your singleness grow closer to the Father by way of prayer; in opening those communications for this single season in your life; taping into the Holy Spirit. It is my prayer that these words will help you feel more comfortable in praying to God in all aspects of your life with no doubt, fear, hesitation and with only Godly expectations in you hearing from Him. If you are single due to no longer being married, divorced, widowed, estrangement, haven't yet found and still praying for your Godly mate or just decided to be single for the Father, this book will help you in all those circumstances to cry out to God, right where you are in your singleness.

May God bless you in your walk with Him and it is my hope that this book will be a true blessing to you in helping you to keep those lines of communications open to the Father!

Phillippians 4:6,7

Be careful for nothing but in everything by prayer and supplication with thanksgiving let your requests be made known unto God and the peace of God which passeth all understanding, shall keep your hearts and minds through Christ Jesus.

Psalm 116:2

Because he hath inclined his ear unto me, therefore will I call upon him as long as I live.

About The Author

Refreshing, transparent, bible based, spirit filled. This author was born in the Midwest with old school "midwestern values" and was able to survive molestation, abuse, assaults, several rape attempts, and incarceration, along with the every day challenges that come with being a single mother. God's grace and love has turned her life and experiences into a gift with a passion for single women in Christ. Being single over 40 years both in and out of Christ, she gives a Godly perspective of what being single in Jesus looks like in today's world and what the Word of God has to say to single women about it all. She is answering God's call on her singleness to share experiences with you so you too can find clarity, wisdom, hope and God's "special" love for you and God's plan for this single season in your life. Her love and God's love is for you! Enjoy her Single Ladies in Christ series written just for you.

Dedication

This book is dedicated to my Heavenly Father; so grateful for His mercies unto me that are new everyday, and for sending the Holy Spirit and the Word to write this book with me. So humbled to be used to share His blessings. Also to my mother, who is in heaven watching my every move, without whose strength and Godly prayers on my behalf, I would have not made it this far, and also to my son and his beautiful family for their unconditional love. So grateful they love me just as I am! Love you all so much!!

Contents

Chapter 1   Prayer for Being Alone 1

Chapter 2   Prayer for A Godly but Broken Single Heart 5

Chapter 3   Prayer for the Single Godly Widow's Heart 9

Chapter 4   Prayer for Keeping My Temple................13

Chapter 5   Prayer for A Single Girls Career/Workday/ Workplace..17

Chapter 6   Single Girls Prayer for My Financial Stability 21

Chapter 7   Single Girls Prayer for Her Family 25

Chapter 8   Single Girls Prayer for Finding Godly Companion or In Knowing God's Direction for Your Single Life 29

Chapter 9   Prayer for the Single Mom in Christ 33

Chapter 10   Prayer for My Church and My Community...37

Chapter 11   Prayer for Healing My Body 41

Chapter 12   Prayer and Thanksgiving In ALL My Singleness 45

OR

(in other words, Lord, thankfulness and contentment for my single heart as a result of Bad Marriage, Divorce, Death resulting in my being a Widow, Ex of the Ex, Separation or

Estrangement, Single Mama Drama, Totally and Completely Single Just for You or Thank You Jesus, I never was married)

PRAYER FOR
BEING ALONE

Matthew 28:19, 20 (KJV)

Go ye therefore and teach all nations, baptizing them in the name of the Father, and of the Son and of the Holy Ghost! Teaching them to observe all things whatsoever I have commanded you; and lo, I am with you always, even unto the end of the world. Amen.

My heart is broken and I am so afraid of being alone that I find myself sometimes willing to settle and willing to compromise your word, for I am weak. Your word, though tells me that when I am at my weakest, you are at your strongest and I have faith in your word! Help me to have the self confidence, trust and faith in you to stand on your promise that you will mend my broken heart and dispel all fear.

I take authority in knowing that you will not leave me or forsake me! That you have left me a Comforter in the Holy Spirit to help me through those restless, lonely times. Help me to know that you did not give me a spirit of fear of being lonely. That fear is from the enemy and I take the authority to cancel that assignment of fear in my life.

Separate me from any unhealthy relationship or habit that separates me from You!

Help me to wait on you to send me a mate in my life and to **not** look to my own means just for the sake of not being by myself. I deserve the best and am willing to wait and trust your judgment in providing the best circumstances for my life.* Fill my life with overflowing love for You and to help put You and only You as first in every area of my single life.

In the precious name of Jesus I pray, Amen

*It takes a great amount of courage for a single women to follow God and not to compromise or settle, but God gives us the strength to do it! In Him all things are possible!

Prayer for A Godly but Broken Single Heart

Phillipians 4:6, 7 (KJV)

Be careful for nothing; but in every thing by prayer and supplication with thanksgiving, let your requests be made known unto God. And the peace of God, which passeth all understanding, shall keep your hearts and minds through Christ Jesus.

Lord, You know my heart. You know my circumstances. You said You would forgive my sins as far as the east is from the west. Shame, guilt, low self esteem, pride, fear, apprehension, selfishness – change my heart; change my mind. Help me to fill my heart with pure, holy, Godly things; help me to be more Christlike. I trade my ashes for your beauty. Increase my faith. Give me a spirit to know that you will be there to help me in all situations. Help me to embrace Your Word and Your promises unto me.

Put people in my way that know You and Your Word and work thru them to console me when needed. Bless them Lord. Bring to my heart a closer walk in

You and a forgiveness, peace, love and contentment that surpasses all understanding. Heal every part of my brokenness and help me to see You and You only so I can rest in You and Your joy and blessings for my life. In Jesus name I pray, Amen.

PRAYER FOR THE SINGLE GODLY WIDOW'S HEART

James 1:27 (KJV)

Pure religion and undefiled before God and the Father is this, to visit the fatherless and widows in their affliction and to keep him unspotted from the world.

Dear God,

Help me in this single season of my life. My mate has past and my heart feels sometimes lonely, torn and broken. Remind me of your promise to me in Psalms 34 that you are nigh unto them that are of a broken heart and a crushed spirit; remind me of how in the Word you have direction to the Children of God how they are to be mindful of me; lifting me up in prayer, visiting with me, showing compassion for me. I should never doubt that I hold a special place in your heart. Keep me, strengthen me, revive my single spirit now to continue to place you first in honor and glory and help me also to be a blessing to others; shining your light wherever I go. In Jesus name, Amen.

PRAYER FOR KEEPING MY TEMPLE

I Corinthians 6:19, 20 (KJV)

What know ye not that your body is the temple of the HolyGhost which is in you, which ye have of God and ye are not your own? For ye are bought with a price: therefore glorify God in your body, and in your spirit which are God's.

Dear Father,

Give me wisdom and clarity on Your will for my body; Your temple. No matter what the world may say; no matter what friends and family may say, help me to make priority in my life, Your Word and what You say about my habits, lifestyle and how I carry my body and how I will wait until marriage to show my physical passion for someone; Lord and if your will is not marriage for my life, help me to accept that as well.

Help me to display the fruits of the sprit in handling my body and displaying those fruits in a humbling, holy way that honors You. Remind me that you want nothing but the BEST FOR ME and that with those thoughts in mind, I can wait on Your BEST for my life and not to consider a physical or emotional compromise in my singleness. Strengthen me, Lord. Reassure me of my first Love, You Father.

All these things I ask in Jesus name, Amen.

Prayer for a Single Girls Career/Workday/ Workplace

Matthew 5:16 (KJV)

Let your light so shine before men, that they may see your good works, and glorify your Father which is in heaven.

Father, thank You for good work! Sometimes I don't feel like work, but Lord help me to reflect you in all I do, including when I am in the workplace doing my everyday job. For God Your Word says that I am in the world, but not of the world. Remind me to keep You first and family and work second. Help me to have the greatest impact for You in spending my work time wisely, my talents and Godly gifts.

Thank You for providing work to give blessings and to be used by You for Your glory. Use me as a calming force in a dark place and to see my coworkers and their needs as you see them.

Create opportunities to counsel, show your love, provide patience and understanding. Help me to see coworkers as more than just people performing tasks that need to be completed. Help me to be a Godly leader; a leader for you, concerned more about people and their needs than performing the tasks at hand. Help me to offer my God given gifts as solutions and help in the workplace. Help me to lead others to you in the workplace and every place I go and to never forget the larger picture, which is You!

In the precious name of Jesus I pray, Amen.

SINGLE GIRLS PRAYER FOR MY FINANCIAL STABILITY

Malachi 3:10 (KJV)

Bring ye all the tithes into the storehouse, that there may be meat in mine house and prove me now herewith, said the Lord of hosts, if I will not open you the windows of heaven and pour you out a blessing and there shall not be room enough to receive it.

God, thank You for my wages, and help me to depend on You in this area of my life! Singleness sometimes would have me to lean on myself for provision and doing what I have to do to make things work; to make ends meet; leaning and depending on myself. Lord take charge of very aspect of my life and that includes my personal finances. Help me not to chase after You for my blessing; in doing what is comfortable in the natural to attempt to remedy my own financial circumstances and then to impatiently wait on a blessing in doing so.

Help me to have faith in the Your supernatural provision and Your promise to provide for me as part of my inheritance as being a Child of the King. Help me to be obedient in giving my tithes, offerings and alms unto Your good works. Prepare my heart to be still and embrace the peace of sowing a good seed and planting it in Your Kingdom and in return being a good stewart of Your harvest; helping to bless others thru Your blessings unto me. Help me always to have a giving heart and help those that are less fortunate than myself. Give me compassion for them and a servant's heart. I pray that I will always have good work and to give cheerfully unto You and Your purposes. In the precious name of Jesus, I pray, Amen.

SINGLE GIRLS PRAYER FOR HER FAMILY

Deuteronomy 6: 5 - 7 (KJV)

And thou shalt love the Lord thy God with all thine heart, and with all thy soul, and with all thy might. And these words, which I command thee this day, shall be in thine heart: And thou shalt teach them diligently unto thy children, and shalt talk of them when thou sittest in thine house, and when thou walkest by the way and when thou liest down and when thou risest up.

Thank You, Lord for my family! Use me, Lord to stand in the gap for them; my children and other family members, those that have accepted you as their Lord and those yet to see You as their Savior. Those that are being influenced by the enemy in their life, keep them safe until they see the realization of Your love and sacrifice for them and come to You to be saved and forgiven. Keep us healthy and strong and help us to make good decisions as we mature to lead a healthy productive life reflecting our blessings from You.

I take authority in the name of Jesus to cancel the enemy's assignment of any generational curses of anger, bitterness, guilt, pride, depression, unforgiveness, addiction and all other dysfunction be broken and help us in the family that have You in our heart, to show Your love, patience and forgiveness. Help us to see them thru your eyes and may they see You thru us! May our family in generations to come, know of You through us that know You now. Save them in our family that don't know you! Cover them in the blood of Jesus, Father. Fill my family's hearts with You!

Teach us all to respect our mothers and fathers so that Your promise of having a long life will be fulfilled. Teach my family to be deep rooted in You. Thank you, Father for all blessings that flow from You!

All these things I ask in the precious name of Jesus, Amen

SINGLE GIRLS PRAYER FOR FINDING GODLY COMPANION OR IN KNOWING GOD'S DIRECTION FOR YOUR SINGLE LIFE

II Corinthians 6:14, 16 - 18 (KJV)

Be ye not unequally yoked together with unbelievers; for what fellowship hath righteousness and unrighteousness? And what communion hath light with darkness? ...And what agreement hath the temple of God with idols? For ye are the temple of the living God; as God hath said, I will dwell in them, and walk in them; and I will be their God and they shall be my people. Wherefore come from among them, and be ye separate, saith the Lords, and touch not the unclean thing; and I will receive you, And will be a Father unto you and ye shall be my sons and daughters, saith the Lord Almighty.

Psalm 119:105 (KJV)

Thy word is a lamp unto my feet and a light unto my path.

Prayers for the Heart of the Single Godly Woman
Single Girls Prayer for Finding Godly Companion or In Knowing God's
Direction for Your Single Life

Dear Heavenly Father, I need Your help in finding a Godly mate, a life time partner who loves You first and would love me second! God direct my steps to meet someone that can only be provided to me by You! Someone who values my spiritual self as well as my physical. Someone who would hold your standards and Word above all else and listens with the same passion and concern that can only come from above. Help me to remember to put You first also in all things.

God if it be Your will that I remain single, direct my path and help me in my "single assignment" to be a blessing to others for You. Help me to accept and embrace my singleness in You and hide Your Word in my heart so that I'll know Your path for my life. Strengthen me for this assignment as only You can, Lord! Mold and make me just for You, Lord! Comfort and keep me. Direct my steps into the future days of my life whatever Your plan may be for me.

Give me clarity, understanding, acceptance and contentment in what You would have for me. Help me to have confidence in knowing that whatever You would have for me and my life, is the best for me and my life, for You created me and You love me. Help me to be reminded again and again, that You have nothing but the BEST FOR ME! There is nothing but goodness in you. In Jesus name I pray, Amen.

PRAYER FOR THE SINGLE MOM IN CHRIST

Phillipians 4:19 (KJV)

But my God shall supply all your needs according to his riches in glory by Christ Jesus.

Thank you God for being my rock and my shield! God help my loneliness in my singleness and provide provision for me and my family. Even though I am the sole parent in the family, reassure my heart that I am your child, You are my Father and my Provider, Yahweh Yireh!

Teach me to rely on you and to have faith in your Word and Your promises. I can rest and find peace in You.

Reassure me in knowing that eventhough I might be what is termed a "single mom" as the world may see me, let me know through the sweet whisper of the Holy Spirit that I am NOT alone on my path through life. Help me to blossom right where I am for You and through You. Watch over me and my family with Your protection as we come and as we go. Teach me to lean and trust on You first and in Your abilities and power in my life and not to lean to my own single strength to provide or to attempt to understand Your ways.

In the precious name of Jesus I pray, Amen.

Use this psalm, single sister, to soothe your soul:

Psalm 23 (KJV)

The Lord is my shepherd; I shall not want

He maketh me to lie down in green pastures; he leadeth me beside the still waters.

He restoreth my soul; he leadeth me in the paths of righteousness for his name's sake

Yea, though I walk through the valley of the shadow of death, I will fear no evil: for thou art with me; thy rod and thy staff they comfort me.

Thou preparest a table before me in the presence of mine enemies: thou anointest my head with oil; my cup runneth over.

Surely goodness and mercy shall follow me all the days of my life: and I will dwell in the house of the Lord for ever.

PRAYER FOR MY CHURCH AND MY COMMUNITY

Hebrews 10:24 – 25 (KJV)

And let us consider one another to provoke unto love and to good works: Not forsaking the assembling of ourselves together, as the manner of some is; but exhorting one another; and so much the more, as ye see the day approaching.

God I am lifting up my Church to You for blessings for the pastors, the ministries, the members and for the community and for all the good Word taught and miracles done and prayers and praises gone up in that place unto You.

Help us to always be reminded that the church is more than a building, but it serves as a gathering place for people that love You and to worship and praise You; a place to offer hope of a new life and a new beginnings in You. A place to give thanks and to bring our tithes and offerings so they can be blessed as "good seed" to be planted to further help to spread the good new of You.

Remind us that the Church is the body of Christ which was purchased by the blood of Jesus and to serve the community in your name; bringing and spreading the gospel and proving Your Light and Your Love to those in need; Help them not to see us but to see You. As Jesus welcomed all, help my church to welcome all as well to experience Your love, your healing and your amazing deliverance and saving grace and Your plan for their lives; to be able to offer real Godly tools for living in a real world that does not put You first.

Give the Pastors and leaders strength, fortitude and vision to further your Word and Your purpose. Bless them all richly for all they do. Revive their spirit and rejuvenate their calling! Uphold them with Your Righteous Right Hand!

Help this church to reflect you in all that it does both in the church building and outside in the community. Holy Spirit you are welcome in my church! In Jesus precious name I pray, Amen.

PRAYER FOR
HEALING MY BODY

Psalm 103: 1 – 5 (KJV)

Bless the Lord, O my soul: and all that is within me, bless his holy name. Bless the Lord, O my soul, and forget not all his benefits: Who forgiveth all thine iniquities; who healeth all thy diseases; Who redeemeth thy life from destruction; who crowneth thee with lovingkindness and tender mercies;...

Proverbs 4: 20 – 22 (KJV)

My son, attend to my words; incline thine ear unto my saying. Let them not depart from thine eyes; keep them in the midst of thine heart. For they are life unto those that find them, and health to all their flesh.

Heavenly Father, you said that Your Word is life to those who find it and medicine to all their flesh. Help me to embrace your Word and hide it in my single heart and to be healed!

In our modern world, Lord, doctors are fine; they're blessed and often times You use them to work to administer to our physical bodies, but help me also not to judge by my eyes but by thy Word and let You attend to my spirit and my single heart. Help me to remember that You have the final word!

Psalm 103: 3 states that you forgave all my sins and healed all my diseases. I take authority over the enemy's assignment on my body and I speak healing into my body in the name of Jesus! Heal me totally and completely, Lord. Keep me healthy to further Your cause and Your assignment on my heart; help me to honor my temple with healthy habits that honor You and Your Word.

In the precious name of Jesus I pray, Amen.

Prayer and Thanksgiving In ALL My Singleness

OR

(in other words, Lord, thankfulness and contentment for my single heart as a result of Bad Marriage, Divorce, Death resulting in my being a Widow, Ex of the Ex, Separation or Estrangement, Single Mama Drama, Totally and Completely Single Just for You or Thank You Jesus, I never was married)

I Thessalonians 5:18 (KJV)

In everything give thanks: for this is the will of God in Christ Jesus concerning you.

Phillipians 4:6, 7 (KJV)

Be careful for nothing; but in everything by prayer and supplication with thanksgiving, let your requests be made known unto God. And the peace which passeth all understanding shall keep your hearts and minds through Christ Jesus.

My God, I bring my single heart to You with thanksgiving for covering me in Your Blood and protecting me. Thank you for wisdom and clarity in all that I have learned in being single.

Keep me, Lord in the palm of your hand and remind me that in Your Word, You said that no man can pluck me out of your hand and there is no where I can be that Your love cannot reach me! You provide a safe place for me; You provide a loving place for me; You provide a healing place for me; You provide a peaceful place for me; You provide a joyful place for me.

I could never thank you enough for saving me and keeping me and allowing me the privilege to serve and represent You in all I do! I Love You!

Thank you for blessing me to allow me to be a blessing to others. In Jesus name, Amen.

Reference Page

All bible scriptures in text taken from the Holy Bible, Old and New Testaments in the King James Version translated out of the Original Tongues and with Previous Translations Diligently Compared and Revised Self-Pronouncing, Words of Christ in Red, with Red-along References, Red-along Translations Thomas Nelson Publishers, Nashville Copyright 1976 by Thomas Nelson, Inc. Nashville, Tennessee

Printed in the United States
By Bookmasters